Within the walls of this book of poetry you will find:

Faith to sustain you
Hope for the future
Genuine love
Lasting friendship

So open read and absorb the goodness of God.

SHARED THOUGHTS AND FEELINGS

A Book of Poems

Published by Writers House Publishing
© 2017 All rights reserved.

SHARED THOUGHTS AND FEELINGS
ISBN 978-0-9986072-1-4

Printed in the United States of America.

All scripture references and quotations, unless otherwise indicated, are taken from the
Holy Bible – King James Version

Book Cover by Aubie Gene Norris
Book Production and Graphics by:
Writers House Publishing

FOREWORD

And here's one more way that poetry is like music. It's said that people's favorite tune is the one most popular when they first fell seriously in love—though probably everything surrounding such a moment remains memorable. It has to do with what enthralls the heart. So too, with poems. Our allegiances are formed by our first serious readings—the poems we get that speak to the heart. I don't mean childhood rhymes or classroom assignments given by our high school reading teachers. I mean those few poems that you parsed and plumbed, dazzled by their knowledge of your very soul. They are usually slightly elliptical: what we cannot grasp is the mystery that draws us in. The problem is that these poems block out others. Friends with discerning tastes and heightened intelligences, when discussing poetry with their peers, inevitably return to the early poem they have admired for years.

Sis Carmen Howard has been a great inspiration to me since I was a small child. She encouraged me every moment she got. I can say her poetry has been some of the most inspiring pieces I've ever heard. I admire her relationship with God as she seeks him to get direction in her writings. I'm blessed to say I know you and even more honored to share in this poetry journey.

Your new Pastor, Jason F. Meachum

How I Spend My Quiet Time

The Bible is a guide from Genesis to Revelation. It provides directives towards a better way of living. One morning I was traveling to work by way of the Metro bus line. I had just finished reading Romans, chapter 5 and 6. I sat near a window looking out and reflecting on the message. I considered it's meaning as it related to my own life and thought, "if only I had known." Within me emanated the soft whisper of a voice that said: "write what you feel," and I did. I wrote my first poem. Since that day, I've often spent my quiet moments writing poetry. Scriptures became my greatest inspiration and therefore, accompany each piece of my writings.

Genesis 28:16b
Surely the Lord is in this place and I knew it not.

If Only I Had Known

If only I had known the love of God
If only I had known the goodness of Jesus
If only I had known the peace of the Holy Spirit
How much happier I would have been
If only I had known the difference between luck and grace
If only I had known the meaning of God's word
If only I had sought the kingdom of God
How much happier I would have been
So seek ye first the kingdom of God
And all its righteousness
Just remember the wages of sin is death
And the gift of our Lord is the best

Romans 5:19
For as by one man's disobedience many were made sinners,
So by the obedience of one shall many be made righteous.

"That was the beginning of "Shared Thoughts and Feelings"

I

Psalms 119:105
Thy word is a lamp unto my feet, and a light unto my path.

The written word of God is a path one must be willing to follow. It all stems from the living word, Jesus Christ, the Son of God. Allow Him to lead you. We are at liberty to receive God's love, grace, and mercy. Believe, have faith and trust in the word of God. Jesus says:

Matthew 6:33
But seek ye first the kingdom of God, and his
righteousness; and all these things will be added unto you.

Sometimes we face problems without solutions, regarding family matters, finances, and health issues. Although we worry, prayer is the key. Prayer is the solution. God's spirit endows us with divine peace during those challenging moments. The results may not always concur with our ideas, but it becomes the most suitable for the nature of our problems.

Matthew 5:16
Let your light so shine before men, that they may see your good works,
And glorify your father which is in heaven.

Life's challenges allow us to relate to one another. Our experiences justify our ability to aid one another. Our hope in God is our deliverance, which reveals His glory. We are also supposed to encourage one another and in order to do that, we need to know what we are talking about. Consider who brought you out of your situation, allowing your light to shine. Your mental and physical being is not always enough to bring you through.

Psalms 147:5
Great is our Lord and of great power,
His understanding is infinite.

And during those moments when we feel alone, there is a remedy for that. It's entitled:

The Power Of God

If you're in the cellar of life
and you feel there's no way out
Just talk to God, for He's the one
your life should be about
He sometimes let you sink so low
for He allows you to use your mind
He can also bring you to new heights
when you realize He's one of a kind
He's above all things, He's below all things
He's to your left and to your right
And when you learn to trust in Him
your battles He will fight
So open up your heart and mind
as you live from day to day
Believing our bridge to God is Jesus
and He is our only way

Proverbs 3:5,6
Trust in the Lord with all thine heart
and lean not unto thine own understanding .
In all thy ways acknowledge him,
and he will direct thy paths.

III

It is important that we not only learn God's word but also conceal it in our hearts. We must put on the whole armor of God, and follow His plan for our lives. He has made the way; we just need to know when to walk therein. A friend Rev. Curley Randall once said: "The reason why an orchestra has a conductor is that everyone will know when it's time for them to play their instrument." God's Spirit leads us on how and when to use our gifts. Like the orchestra, know your gift, and pay attention to Christ, our conductor. Those quiet moments with God gives directives on the use of our gifts.

Quiet Moments

The quiet time I spend with God
is the best time of the day
It's in the stillness I always ask
that he will guide my way
My quiet time is spent just thinking
of all he's brought me through
My quiet time is asking the Lord
to also strengthen you
And when those quiet moments pass
and come to an end
He gives me peace and courage
till that quiet time comes again

Proverbs 16:3
Commit thy works unto the Lord and thy thoughts shall be established.

I will always be grateful for the love and sermons of my late Pastors. It was Rev. U.S. Turney who further opened my understanding to God's word and strengthened my belief. His ministry encouraged me to write my second poem.

I Believe

I may not understand all the mysteries of creation
I know there is life and death
I may not understand all about the resurrection
But I believe all things are in God's hands
Hands that reach out and touch a weary heart
From the trials that we have from day to day
Hands that reach out with a gift of joy and love
Our pure and Holy God this is His way
I may not understand how He loves all sinners
I know He is patient and kind
I may not understand how
He can turn us into winners
But I believe all things are in God's hands

Psalms 33:9
For he spake, and it was done; he commanded, and it stood still.

V

Rev. Clifford B. Meachum Jr. gave a sermon on God being greater than great, and again the Holy Spirit inspired me to write.

Better Than The Best

The God I serve is greater than great
That's something we all should know
He's a loving God, a giving God,
He's real, He's not a show
He talks to your heart
through His Holy Spirit
that dwells somewhere within
He lets you know all things are possible,
If you place your trust in Him
The God I serve is richer than rich
All things belong to Him
He gives His love and whatever we need
When we learn to abide in Him
The road gets rough sometimes I know,
and you can't see around the bend
But the God I serve says keep the faith,
We'll be with you till the end
And at the end of your rainbow
you will find much more in store
For the gift of God is eternal life
and Jesus is the door

Proverbs 30:5
Every word of God is pure
He is a shield unto them that put their trust in him.

Pastor Clifford Meachum's motto was "A lot of good can be done, if no one cares who gets the credit."

We now have a new young Pastor, Jason F. Meachum. He is carrying on the legacy of his father, the late Pastor Clifford Meachum Jr. He's young enough to learn and old enough to teach. He has a good message in each sermon. His ministry furthered enabled me to express my thoughts and feelings.

Job 37:2
Hear attentively the noise of his voice
and the sound that goeth out of his mouth.

The Noise Of The World

When you talk and pray to God
Can you hear Him through the noise
When everyone is talking,
Do you recognize His voice
His voice is in His written word,
He tells us how to live
How to treat other people,
as we share and what we give
We should be sharing the word of God,
He sacrificed His Son
We have a chance to follow Him,
and it's intended for everyone
Satan's voice sometimes seems louder
He wants us to be confused
But when we know and follow Christ,
Satan's words will be refused
So when life's noise surrounds you,
and you don't know what to do
Remember God is still the one that's
looking out for you
The voice of God is quiet, but loud enough to hear
So hide His word within your heart,
and know He's always near

Not only am I grateful to the pastors in my life, but also their wives, Sis. Alberta Turney, and Sis. Dorothy Meachum. Their discussions in B.T.U (Baptist Training Union) and Sunday school encouraged me to continue writing as an example to young women. Their training also inspired me to encourage women in support of their husbands. We can learn a lot from each other when we listen with an open mind.

ACKNOWLEDGEMENTS

Of course I must first recognize the Father, Son, and Holy Spirit for without grace and mercy there would be no Shared Thoughts and Feelings by me.

My acknowledgment, I combine with gratitude to everyone who encouraged me. Although I cannot name you all individually, know that you are loved and appreciated. To my eldest son Stephen, his wife Joyce, to my daughter, Marsha, who helps me to stay organized, and Jeffery, my youngest son, I am grateful beyond measure. To my brother Ray Parcee, thank you for keeping my computer up and running. To my brother Dennis Hanks, for the cover photo. To my Starlight M.B. Church family, I value your love. Aubie Gene Norris, your artistry in the design of my book cover is highly appreciated. My publisher, Loretta Norris of Writers House Publishing, you have always believed in me. Alvin and Janice Weaver, the sharing of your love has encouraged me to reach beyond the borders of family, friends, and acquaintances. In doing so, I have received responses and acknowledgments from the White House, and the 44th President of the United States of America, Barack Obama and First Lady Michelle Obama. Finally, to my extended family and faithful friends, I thank you all for your love and support.

DEDICATION

I deeply appreciate everyone who has crossed my path in life, because every encounter has helped me in the creation of my book. I dedicate this book to my mother Virginia, grand-mother, Lena, also known as Grams, my son-in-law Richard Norris Sr. and to my Deanna who are all just waiting for the trumpets to sound.

The following pages bring to life, inspirational thoughts and feelings in which I now share with you. I hope you enjoy reading them as much as I have enjoyed writing them!

TABLE OF CONTENTS

SHARED THOUGHTS AND FEELINGS

SHARED THOUGHTS AND FEELINGS

SHARED
THOUGHTS
AND
FEELINGS

By

Carmen L. Howard

A Christian Under Construction

Ephesians 6:11
Put on the whole armour of God, that ye may be able to
stand against the wiles of the devil

We all are Christians under construction
for we err from day to day
But thanks be to God, who gave us Jesus
through Him we have a new way
A way to live a better life, even though
we have sick days, pain, and strife
For the word of God can bring you out
sometimes we cry, sometimes we shout
But don't you worry, God's word is true
Just try doing better and try to improve
All things are possible, if we take Jesus hand
He prepared for us a perfect new land
And always try to treat your neighbor right
Give God all the glory and continue your fight

Isaiah 26:4
Trust in the Lord forever;
for in the Lord Jehovah is everlasting strength.

A Cry For Blessings And Promise Of Praise

Psalms 145:19
He will fulfill the desires of them that fear him;
He also will hear their cry, and will save them.

Again Lord, You heard my cry
and had pity on my groans
I know as long as I live on this earth
I will look up toward Your throne
And even when I leave this life
since You forgave my sins
I will always be around Your throne
singing praises for there's no end
There's only end to our pain and sorrow
There will always be brighter tomorrows
I'm glad I believe in You and Your words
They're best words that I know
I pray that others around the world
will hear them and spiritually grow
Then we can look at one another
and share the love You give
And be at peace enjoying Your blessings
each day as we live

Psalms 145:9
The Lord is good to all:
and his tender mercies are over all his works.

A Daily Challenge

Psalms 46:1
God is our refuge and strength,
a very present help in trouble

When it seems you've come
to the end of your road
and you don't know what to do
God has a plan already worked out
that will help and comfort you
He put his plan in writing
and we just have to read
So when we say I can't
it will give us what we need
There's a challenge in each day's journey
that will help to make us strong
So when Satan tries to tempt us
we can tell him to move along
Some days may not be easy
sometimes the tears may flow
We still can count on the Father and Son
to know which way to go
As you accept your daily challenge
thank God for being there
Regardless of what you're going through
you know God truly cares

A Firm Foundation

Deuteronomy 6:6,7a
And these words, which I command thee
this day, shall be in thine heart.
And thou shall teach them diligently unto thy children.

A Father is caring
A Father is strong
He will tell his children
when they are right or wrong
He tries to share what he has learned
Especially about the gift
we can never earn
It comes from the Father up above
God's gift of grace, mercy and love
The best thing a Father could ever give
Is sharing with his Children
a gift like this

A Goal Worth Setting

Revelations 21:4
And God shall wipe away all tears from their eyes;
and there shall be no more death, neither sorrow, nor crying,
neither shall there be any more pain:
for the former things have passed away.

As you travel life's journey
have you set yourself a goal
Do you ever thank the Father and Son
For the sacrifice that saved your soul
Do you know what you will say to God
after you close your eyes
Are you treating your neighbors
with love and respect
or listening to Satan's lies
All questions can be answered
if you learn God's written word
But you will never know the answers
if it's something you've never heard
So when you read your bible
don't forget to pray
And ask God's Spirit to guide you
While you're trying to find your way
It's in the promise land where you
will reach your goal
And never be sick, and never grow old

A Helping Hand

Nahum 1:7
The Lord is good, a strong hold in the day of trouble;
and he knoweth them that trust in him.

We all have problems from day to day
Whether they be great or small
We all have a Savior to lead the way
And He's willing to help us all
He stands at the gate
He will open the door
All you have to do is walk in
He will mend your ways
and brighten your days
He will let new life begin
Just hear His words, accept His hand
And let this life flow through
Then thank Him for renewing your mind
And making a brand new you

A Home With The King

Revelations 21:4
And God shall wipe away all tears from their eyes;
and there shall be no more death, neither sorrow,
nor crying, neither shall there be any more pain:
for the former things have passed away.

We never know the month or day
When our life on earth is through
But Jesus says if you follow Him
He will make your life brand new
If you have the faith of a mustard seed
He will open your heart and supply your needs
He will give you joy and peace of mind
No other place this gift you'll find
It's free for those who will take His hand
He will be your guide to a perfect new land
It's something new to look forward to
A perfect home prepared for you
So don't be sad if your loved one has gone
Be encouraged and pray they are heaven bound
To live in peace with no more tears
With the heavenly Father and eternal years
For we never know who He forgives
This gift is not ours it's only His

A Morning Prayer

1 Chronicles 16:23
Sing unto the Lord, all the earth;
shew forth from day to day his salvation.

Lord, let me do the best I can
As I walk along today
Give me your love
and allow me to show
Jesus, you are the way
Help me forgive
let me be fair
Help me to follow you
Let my lifestyle show your life
In everything I try to do

11 Timothy 4:4
And they shall turn away their ears from the truth,
and shall be turned unto fables.

A Mother's Love

11 Corinthians 1:3
Blessed be God, even the Father of our
Lord Jesus Christ, the Father of mercies,
and the God of all comfort.

A mother's love is hard to beat
For they endure their children's heat
Wherever they go, whatever they do
When they turn to Mom
She will help them through
God watches all children day and night
Regardless of their wayward plight
A mother knows her prayers are heard
For her prayers are in
the name of God's living word
(Jesus Christ)

A Need To Turn Around

Malachi 3:7b
Return unto me, and I will return unto you,
saith the Lord of host.

We always seem to start out on the wrong foot
But thanks to our God
He takes a second look
He gives us each day our daily bread
We know blessings come from Him
Because of what we have read
Although in this life We have joy and sorrow
His promise gives us hope for a brighter tomorrow
He sacrificed His only Son as a sign of His love
And His grace and mercy comes from above
The ways of Jesus we should hide in our hearts
It gives us strength for each day a new start
If you're still on the wrong foot just turn around
And thank God for a chance to be Heaven bound

Psalms 46:1
God is our refuge and strength,
a very present help in trouble.

A Prayer For This Day

Psalm 68:19a
Blessed be the Lord,
who daily loadeth us with benefits

This Day I must show love
This Day I must be kind
This Day I pray for strength, for tomorrow
I may be gone
Let me treat my neighbor right
let my heart be filled with joy
Help me do your will today
for tomorrow I may be gone
Give us This Day our daily bread
Forgive my wrong thoughts, or things I've said
Clean me up and make me right
for tomorrow I may be gone
Thank you Lord for all your gifts
Thank you for leading my way
Thank you for your comforting spirit
and the blessings you'll give This Day

According To God's Promise

Galatians 3:28
There is neither Jew nor Greek, there is neither bond nor free, there is
neither male nor female; for ye are all one in Christ Jesus.

Another day's journey has just begun
To give God thanks for His matchless Son
You know His name is Jesus
He died to set us free
But now He reigns by His Father's side
and says we must believe
He knows life is full of anger,
depression, illness, and pain
That's why we have the Bible
to show what we can gain
One day there will be no sickness,
no heartache, or disease
The written word was left for us
to put our minds at ease
So as you start today's journey
with thanksgiving in your heart
Remember, you're one of God's chosen people,
whom He has set apart

Galatians 3:29
And if ye be Christ's, then are ye Abraham's seed,
and heirs ing to the promise.

Along Life's Narrow Way

Psalms 121 :1
I will lift up mine eyes unto the hills,
from whence cometh my help.

When we pray to God in Jesus name
He takes away our fear
He gives us strength and courage
And His Spirit is always near
Our faith is what sustains us
Believing God's word is true
Through all the trials we have in life
He shows us what to do
So keep your head up to the sky
And thank Him every day
Keep praying with your trust in Him
He will guide you the right way

An Introduction

Proverbs 18:24
A man that hath friends, must show himself friendly:
and there is a friend that sticketh closer than a brother.

Let me help you find a friend
One as close as mine
A friend that keeps your confidence
A friend who's always kind
One that sticks through thick and thin
One that's always true
One that has a forgiving heart
No matter what you do
And when you meet this friend of mine
Your ways will surely change
For He will teach you Godly ways
You see, JESUS is His name

An Old Fashioned Mother

III John 1:4
I have no greater joy than to hear that
my children walk in truth.

A mother has the love of God within and without
The way she walks and the way she talks
Leaves a person no doubt
She's a leader and a teacher of the word of God
And rules with a rod of steel
She stumbles through her daily chores
But still can cook a meal
When day is done the night creeps in
When eyes are closed and prayer begins
She thanks her heavenly Father above
For His strength, peace, joy and love

Luke 1:28
And the angel came in unto her and said,
"Hail, thou that art highly favored,
the Lord is with thee. Blessed are thou among women.

Another Gift From God

Proverbs 31:10
Who can find a virtuous woman?
for her price is far above rubies.

A true mother is a gift from God
And all His gifts are precious
He fills her with His tender love
He makes her strong yet gracious
She's always there to fill your needs
Her prayers are always heard
She's able to be a mother to you
Because she follows God's word
And if by chance He's called her home
Because He wanted her there
Lift up your head and thank Him for
The good times that you shared

Another Talk With God

Psalms 66:18
If I regard iniquity in my heart,
the Lord will not hear me.

Father it would be so wonderful
If You could depend on us
To be the people that You made
And You could really trust
Thank You for giving us Jesus
And showing us He's the way
We're able to have some happy times
As we live from day to day
It's up to us to share Your love
With all our Sisters and Brothers
Not only the ones whose names we know
But also many others
So as we try to live this life
Sometime with heartache and pain
When we follow Your written and living word
I know we have much to gain
I ask that You be patient
And keep Your forgiving heart
I thank You for grace and mercy
And a chance for a brand new start

Be Of Good Courage

Psalm 31:24
Be of good courage, and he shall strengthen
your heart, all ye that hope in the Lord

Courage is needed not only today
But as we travel life's narrow highway
Knowing Jesus is how to survive
Trusting Him keeps our faith alive
Being humble and patient
are traits we must keep
Praying to God for His peace while we sleep
And upon arising to another day
Ask God for His courage
and keep walking His way

Because Of The Cross

I Corinthians 2:9
But it is written, Eye hath not seen, nor ear heard,
neither have entered into the heart of man,
the things which God hath prepared for them that love him.

Because of the Cross we bear our burdens
Though no one likes heartache or pain
But what Jesus did on Calvary
Gives us a chance to gain
A place of peace and harmony
Where we will praise God everyday
Because of the Cross we have this gift
From God's Son who made our way
We may not like what life throws at us
But the Father and Son we still can trust
His Holy Spirit is still our guide
He's always present and by our side
So Because of the Cross we're able to be
Among people who will witness
What God wants us to see
It's not hard to follow Jesus' example
The life He lived was a perfect sample

Ephesians 2:18
For through him we both have access
by one Spirit unto the Father

19

Being A Strong Woman

Proverbs 14:1a
Every wise woman buildeth her house;

A strong woman doesn't have to be like a man
Just stay in her lane and do what she can
With everyday issues, the pain and strife
She keeps moving forward to improve her life
A woman of God must come first
Help from Him lets her deal with the worst
It's good to know a woman can be
The backbone and strength for her family
There's nothing wrong with shedding some tears
It helps get rid of some things she might fear
Jesus our Savior who leads the way
Gave us His Spirit to brighten our days
She lives each day one by one
And is always grateful to God's only Son
The real love He showed on Calvary
Is the kind she gives to her friends and family

Proverbs 14:33a
Wisdom resteth in the heart of him that hath understanding;

Bless Our God

Psalm 66:8
O bless our God, ye people,
and make the voice of his praise be heard.

Hallelujah, praise and glory
I just want to bless Your name
You've given me real life and so much more
I want to tell everyone it's You I adore
When I hear a song or read Your word
In my silent time Your voice is heard
My heart is light, my mind is free
It's then in prayer I give thanks to Thee
If I don't tell it, If I don't show it
If I don't live it, then I'll be the blame
For not sharing that Jesus, God's only Son
Is the way out of sin and shame
So blessings and glory to the Father above,
And His Son by His right hand
For showing true love
For His comforting Spirit so kind and true
He's the guide that was left for me and you

Celebrating The Love Of God

I1 Peter 3:8
Finally, be ye all of one mind,
having compassion one of another,
love as brethren, be pitiful, be courteous.

We celebrate different holidays
And let others know they're loved
But everyday we should share God's love
That's showered from above
If we are kind to one another
Treat each other as Sisters and Brothers
The world would be a better place
To appreciate God's mercy and His grace
So let us strive and look ahead
To the promise of God we've already read
The gift that's offered of eternal life
Where there will be no heartache pain or strife
I'm sending these words so you will feel
The love of God that's lasting and real
Keep holding on to His unchanging hand
It will keep you on the right path
To our perfect new land

Creating A Brighter Tomorrow

Ephesians 6:11
Put on the whole armour of God,
that ye may be able to stand
against the wiles of the devil

When our dreams are focused on Jesus
It makes for a brighter tomorrow
For He tells about the paths you can choose
Whether they be broad or narrow
We all have our thoughts and feelings
That can change from day to day
But we learn Jesus gave His life for us
To make a better way
A way to a wholesome meaningful life
Even though we have heartache pain and strife
It's how you think and what you do
That creates a life that's full and new
All things are possible if you believe
That our Father above can supply your needs
Our wants are not always good for us
But the love of God you can always trust
When you open your eyes every morning
Thank God and bless His name
Be sure to put on all His armor
It helps you through life's worldly games

Enjoy Each Day
(Of God's Blessings)

2 Timothy 4:8
Henceforth there is laid up for me a crown
of righteousness which the Lord, the righteous judge,
shall give me at that day, and not to me only,
but unto all them also that love his appearing,

Take time for yourself, appreciate your friend
The friend that can help when life seems to bend
Take time for yourself, enjoy what you do
For each day you live is different and new

Sometimes valleys are low, you feel despair
Your road seems to end, and no one cares
But with each new day, God gives a new choice
And allows us to lift up our hands and rejoice

So thanks be to God for His mercy and grace
Just ask Him for strength to continue your race
Then keep on running, don't turn around
For the one that endures,
receives that promised crown

Exhortation To Praise

Psalm 107:1
O give thanks unto the Lord, for he is good;
for his mercy endureth forever

Lord as often as I say thank you
it's not enough for me
For You have shown me many things
my eyes just could not see
The beauty all around me
the love that's deep within
The wonderful gift of Your grace and mercy
Even though we all have sinned
I pray for my friends and loved ones
I pray You make them strong
I pray for others around the world
even if their lifestyle is wrong
I thank You again for waking me up
and starting a brand new day
Special thanks for Your darling Son Jesus
and showing us He is the way
To a place you've prepared and opened the door
Where we'll find new life and so much more

Expecting Better Days

Psalm 8:9
O Lord our Lord, how excellent
is thy name in all the earth.

We ask the Lord to pass us not
to hear us when we cry
He soothes our troubled hearts
and then, we want to ask Him why
Why did I have to go through
all the heartache and pain?
Why does it seem my life is filled
with cloudy days and rain?
Even when the clouds pass by
and you're stronger than before
God continues to show His kindness
and blesses us even more
So when you have your questions
remember God knows what's best
And keep in mind our life on earth
is sometimes just a test
Our best days lie ahead of us
when we reach that land above
And really know the meaning of
a genuine true love

John 10:9
I am the door; by me if any man enter in, he shall be saved,
and shall go in and out and find pasture.

Faith

11 Corinthians 5:7
For we walk by faith and not by sight

Faith has been known as a healing force
A thing you're unable to see
Faith can lead you through trying times
God says, if you believe in me
Faith gives your life richness
Faith supplies patience
Faith gives you a reason to live
Trusting that Jesus can bind you to God
And believing it's His gift to give.

Psalms 18:2
The Lord is my rock, and my fortress, and my deliverer; my God,
my strength, in whom I will trust; my buckler,
and the horn of my salvation, and my high tower.

Father In Heaven

Psalms 18:32
It is God that girdeth me with strenght, and maketh my way perfect.

As I start a new day where you made a way
All I can do is say thank you
Even in my pain I know there's much to gain
So I still have to say thank you
Thank you for the plan you made
Knowing we all would go astray
You gave us your only begotten Son
Who shed His blood for everyone
He died on the cross but all was not lost
So again I have to say thank you
No longer on earth but He left us a guide
Your Holy Spirit stays by our side
Through all of life's issues He allows us to know
If we listen to Him we'll see which way to go
With Your patience, love, mercy and grace
We have another day to continue our race
And look to the hills where our help comes from
So again I have to say thank you!

Psalms 22:50
Therefore I will give thanks unto thee,
O Lord, and I will sing praises unto thy name.

Finding Life's Treasures

Psalm 32:8
I will instruct thee and teach thee in the way which thou shalt go:
I will guide thee with mine eye.

Our lives can be filled with happy times
If we put away foolish things
And look to the hills
From which cometh our help,
And accept the joy it brings
Life can be like a roller coaster
full of highs and lows
But when we follow the word of God
He will minimize all our woes
Jesus is our shepherd
God's only obedient Son
He died on the cross to save our souls
And He did it for everyone
God tells us in His written word
all that we must do
We only have to accept his offer
And He'll make our lives brand new

Proverbs 20:27
The spirit of man is the candle of the Lord,
searching all the inward parts of the belly.

29

For All He's Done For Us

Revelation 4:11
Thou art worthy, O Lord, to receive glory and honour and power; for thou
hast created all things, and for thy pleasure they are and were created.

Our Creator gave two eyes to see
He gave two ears as well
One mouth to talk to others
One nose so we could smell
Two arms to do the work we need
Two legs to get around
Let's not forget our hands and feet
and our face to smile and frown
He put a heart within us
to feel and share His love
A love that we could never match
true love from up above
God gave his Son to show us
how sacrifice is made
He knew we needed special help
so our souls could be saved
We should always be grateful
for He has much more in store
He gave His Son Jesus power
and the keys that unlock the door
The only door we must go through
it leads to our heavenly home that's new

Revelation 3:21
To him that over cometh will I grant to sit at thy feet with me in my
throne, even as I also overcame, am sit down with my father in His throne.

Forging Ahead

James 4:7
Submit yourselves therefore to God.
Resist the devil and he will flee from you.

Left foot right foot we learn how to walk
Mama Daddy we learn how to talk
Going to school we learn how to read
Reading our Bibles we learn about good deeds
Deeds by God our Father and His only Son
They showed us how two people interact as one
If we could love our Neighbors
The world would be a better place
But since it's in the shape it's in
Thank God for mercy and grace
What we do for Christ will last
So live your new life and not your past
As we give our lives to Jesus
He will forgive us all
For on His list of people
there is no great or small

Colossians 3:16a
Let the word of Christ dwell in you richly in all wisdom;

Fulfilling Your Lives Together

Hebrews 13:16
But to do good and to communicate forget not;
for with such sacrifices God is well pleased.

Your journey in life has just begun
Through ups and downs remember you're one
Life will be different this you know
But with Christ in your life together you'll grow
There's all kind of issues you will face
And you'll get through them
with God's mercy and grace
It's not very hard to say I do
Don't let other voices discourage you
So as you take your sacred vows
Today is the beginning of here and now
But through the word of God you'll see
Your lives can be happy if you believe
If you treat one another as a gift from above
Your marriage will be filled with genuine love

Getting Through Issues Of Life

Psalms 16:1
Preserve me, O God,
for in thee do I put my trust

We may have a lot of stress, and pain
We can't give up, for there's much to gain
Jesus still sits by our Father's side
His Holy Spirit is still our guide
We must stay strong, no matter what
For Satan is there to grab us up
He will try to keep us in a life of sin
So our gift of salvation, we could never win
We need to keep God's word and love alive
And let others know
it's the way to survive
So as we travel along life's road
Following Jesus we've already been told
That through all life's issues, the ups and downs
We shall come forth as pure gold

Revelation 7:14b
These are they which came out of
great tribulation, and have washed their robes,
and made them white in the blood of the Lamb

God Answers Prayer

1 Peter 3:12a
For the eyes of the Lord are over the righteous,
and his ears are open unto their prayers:

I pray for you, you pray for me
That God will give us what we need
The answer may not come right away
But we will have blessings everyday
So hold your faith keep it tight
Keep trusting God He's always right
We may not always understand
But we're able to hold His unchanging hand

God Is Forever

Isaiah 54:8
In a little wrath I hid my face from thee for a moment;
but with everlasting kindness will I have mercy on thee,
saith the Lord thy Redeemer.

When I look around at things today
I say nothing is forever
If we did not have Jesus on our side
we would be lost forever
But God had a plan for woman and man
a chance to change our lives
To have contentment and peace of mind
even with heartache and strife
I've learned when we pray and have faith in Him
He will mend our ways
With all of His grace and undeserved mercy
He will brighten our days
Some prayers are answered right away
sometimes it takes awhile
But through the wait He gives you strength
that even let's you smile
So hold on to your Bible
and read what lies within
It tells you how to live each day
and how it should begin

St. John 6:40
And this is the will of Him that sent me, that everyone that seeth the Son
and believeth on him, may have everlasting life:
and I will raise him up in the last day.

God Is Still In Control

Psalms 121:1,2
I will lift up mine eyes unto the hills, from whence cometh my help. My
help cometh from the Lord, which made heaven and earth.

Regardless of pain and strife in your life
God is still in control
Things may not seem fair as you travel on
But our outcome has been foretold
It's all in the written word of God
His son and those who followed Him
They did not always understand
And we are just like them
You can become bitter and say why me
And throw your hands in the air
But things can get better if you believe
God is not sleep He's aware
His Holy Spirit was left for us
To help soothe our weary minds
Take a deep breath and let others know
This to shall pass in time
If Jesus endured the pain of the cross
To show His love for us
Then we should be able to endure life's issues
And say in God I still trust

I Corinthians 2:5
That your faith should not stand in the wisdom of man,
but in the power of God.

God Looks Beyond The Surface

1 Samuel 16:7b
For the Lord seeth not as man seeth;
for man looketh on the outward appearance,
but the Lord looketh on the heart.

We never know what other people say
When they talk to the Father above
They may be asking for grace and mercy
Even God's unmerited love
Their choices to us may not be the best
But down the line they may pass their test
We only see the outside of man
but God can see within
The heart, mind, and compassion
that can keep us from our sin
None of us are perfect, perfection set us free
When he gave His life for all of us
and died on Calvary
He now sits by His Father's side
and continues to plead our case
He left His Spirit to guide us
while we run our earthly race
So let us try to do our best and help one another
For God is pleased to see us sharing his word
with our sisters and brothers

God's Gift

Psalm124:8
Our help is in the name of the Lord,
who made heaven and earth

When we open our eyes every morning
We know it's a gift from God
There's no other way to start a day
Without this gift from God
His gift lets us love our neighbors
Shows us how to be a friend
Teaches us how to walk and talk
In this world full of sin
There's no other gift so precious
that's received from day to day
Than the gift of God
from Heaven through Christ
that keeps us from going astray

God's Loving, Peaceful Ways
(We Should Share)

Matthew 5:9
Blessed are the peacemakers;
for they shall be called the children of God,
which made heaven and earth.

Amazing is our loving God
His Son and Spirit too
He lifts us up forgives our sins
When He sees we're trying to improve
Although sometime we have pain and sorrow
He gives us hope for a brighter tomorrow
Some days we have rain but the sun will shine again
And it's good to know we have Jesus as a friend
He gave His life to set us free
with a chance to live eternally
So thank him and our Father above
For showing us the meaning of Godly love
A love and peace meant for us to share
To let others know we also care

Mark 9:50B
Have salt in yourselves, and have peace one with another.

God's Strength Sustains Us

Psalms 121:1
I will lift up mine eyes unto the hills,
from whence cometh my help

Sometimes life can throw a curve
That takes your strength away
For in this life are many things
That can make you go astray
Some people look at others
Just to find something wrong
But being in the word of God
Is the thing that keeps us strong
Jesus is the one we should follow
As we look to hills above
The Holy Spirit can guide us
To where we find peace and love
So when that curve is thrown at you
Don't duck just catch the ball
Pick up God's word you'll find what you need
That gives you strength to keep walking tall

Isaiah 26:4
Trust in the Lord forever;
for in the Lord JEHOVAH is everlasting strength

God's Unexpected Blessings

Romans 3:23
For all have sinned, and come short
of the glory of God.

Satan had me for several years
I thought I was happy yet shedding tears
Then I told God I can't do this thing
He said wait my child I have a King
His name is Jesus my only Son
An example of how life's race is won
He taught me the meaning of His word
The best thing that happened or I had heard
It showed me what real love is all about
That's why some of us cry and some of us shout
I never thought that I could be
Useful to God for blessing me
But because of His Son and Spirit too
I'm able to share His love with you

Matthew 5:16
Let your light so shine before men,
that they may see your good works,
and glorify your Father which is in heaven

Growing In The Lord

Psalms 37:5
Commit thy ways unto the Lord; trust also in him;
and he shall bring it to pass.

When you try to come full
circle without Jesus in your life
You go around in circles trying to deal
with your pain and strife
Your choices are not always wise
For you listen to Satan
when he comes disguised
But God had a plan if we only obey
He allowed His Son to be sacrificed
to give us a better way
But first we must be willing
to give up our worldly life
Learn the words of our Father God
and try to do what's right
And you will be surprised how
different your life will become
Then as you go from day to day
you'll see you're having fun
For life in Jesus is never dull
if you manage your time wisely
your circle will be full

Guiding Me Through

1 Peter 5:8
Be sober, be vigilant, because your adversary the Devil, as a roaring
lion walketh about seeking whom he may devour,

Through all these years
Through all my sin and shame
Lord you brought me through
life's worldly games
You opened my eyes so I could see
What our Father's words could mean to me
While trying to do the best I can
I must never forget Satan also has a plan
To keep us from having
God's gift that was given
To keep us from loving
our Savior that's risen
But I know if I stay truly close to you
There's really no damage Satan can do

Ephesians 6:11
Put on the whole armour of God, that ye may be able to stand
against the wiles of the Devil.

Happiness For My Soul

Psalm 57: 7
My heart is fixed, O God, my heart is fixed:
I will sing and give praise

When the lights turn low
and it's time for me to go
Remember God has fixed my soul
There's a place on high where we hurt nor cry
And we never ever grow old
There will be so much to see
We'll praise God continuously
For He's worthy His touch made me whole
Be happy for me for I'll live endlessly
Remember
God has fixed my soul

Psalm 37:18
The Lord knoweth the days of the upright:
and their inheritance shall be forever.

Have A Blessed Day

Psalms 135:5
For I know that the Lord is great,
and that our Lord is above all gods.

Another day the Lord has made
as we travel on our way
I pray that God will bless you
as you live from day to day
We all can live a better life
although there's sickness and pain
There are always better days ahead
when we pray in Jesus name
I hope your day is happy
and filled with peace and love
And remember all good blessings
come from your Father above
I know you may not see Him
but He's always by your side
To give you comfort and let you know
in Him you can abide

Having Faith In God's Word

Hebrews 11:6
But without faith, it is impossible to please him;
for he that cometh to God must believe that he is,
and that he is a rewarder of them that diligently seek him.

Sometimes we take the weight of the world
and put it on our shoulders
When we should leave it in God's hands
He's wiser and He's older
We run around from day to day
always in a hurry
And if we take more time to pray
there would be less time to worry
So take your time look around
enjoy the things you do
Patience can be rewarded
and the Lord will see you through
It may not be how we want it
but God always gives His best
Remember He gave his Son Jesus
who passed all of Satan's tests

Having Good Intentions

Psalms 105:1
O give thanks unto the Lord; call upon his name: make known
his deeds among the people

We should never put off till tomorrow
what we can do today
We may not get a chance to share
the words we want to say
Sharing with somebody
that the word of God is true
Let them know you care about
what they are going through
So take a minute of your day
to see if there's a need
To encourage your brothers and sisters
And wish them both God's speed
You will know you've helped somebody
And brightened up their day
Then give God all the glory
for giving you words to say

Holding God's Hand

James 5:15
And the prayer of faith shall save the sick,
and the Lord shall raise him up; and if
he have committed sins, they shall be forgiven him.

If your prayers are not answered right away
Don't worry help is on the way
For God wants us to have a decent life
Even though we have pain, sorrow, and strife
The Son of God was weary
He even shed some tears
God gave His only begotten Son
a light to shine for years
A light we need to follow
a gift that's kind and true
His Holy Spirit is also near
to tell us what we should do
So as you struggle from day to day
Keep holding on to God's hand
Believing and trusting one day we will be
In that promised perfect new land

Revelations 21:4
And God shall wipe away all tears from their eyes; and there shall be no
more death, neither sorrow nor crying, neither shall there be any more pain:
for the former things are passed away.

Humble Yourself

Mark 10:31
But many that are first shall be last;
and the last first.

If you've spent all your life saying
I, My, Me
It's time to consider God's words and say
You, Us, and We
For He can do the things for you
That man can never do
He sent His Son to save us all
Not just one or two
You need not think that it's too late
For you to change your ways
But do it soon for we never know
The number of our days
So take one step and learn His words
He will take two or more
Keep on seeking keep on knocking
On God's eternal life door.

I Heard The Knock

(And answered the door)

Revelation 3:20
Behold, I stand at the door and knock; if any man hear my voice, and
open the door, I will come in to him, and will sup with him,
and he with me

Thank You Jesus,
my life has been changed
God gave me new life and also a new name
I heard You knock and I opened the door
I learned about true love
and so much more
God's grace and mercy was a great part
But to give His son for sinners was the loving start
I know I'm not perfect
but I treat my neighbors right
I don't try to hide for I'm always in your sight
I'm also glad you are watching
to help guide my way
And keep me strong and focused
when I'm having a bad day
So glory and honor to the Father and Son
Your comforting Spirit, shows us how to run
This race to heaven
or to live on the new earth
Another precious gift given
since we had our new birth

Jude 1:21
Keep yourselves in the love of God, looking for the mercy of our Lord
Jesus Christ unto eternal life.

In God's Sight

John 15:12
This is my commandment, that ye love one another,
as I have loved you.

God is the giver of all good things
Joy and peace is what He brings
He shares His love at all times
A love like His you'll never find
We the people are not precise as
God's matchless Son Jesus Christ
But we should try to do our best
Even when we're under stress
So let your light be seen by others
For in God's sight
We are Sisters and Brothers

In Thee O Lord

Psalm 71:1
In thee, O Lord, do I put my trust.
Let me never be put to confusion.

My God and Jesus my hands stretch to Thee
There's no other help I know
If You should turn your back on me
Your Holy Spirit would also go
I would have no guide from day to day
I would fall off the path that makes my way
Anger and pride would surely come back
With no one to guide me I'd fall through life's cracks

I need Your strength I need Your love
I need all Your blessings sent from above
And what I give You seems so small
Yet You're still there to answer my call
So I thank You with all my heart and mind
For being so patient loving and kind
The thought of You not ever being there
Is more than my heart and mind can bear

Israel's God Is Our God

Galatians 3:8
And the scripture, foreseeing that God would justify the
heathen through faith, preached before the gospel unto Abraham,
saying, In thee shall all nations be blessed.

The God of Abraham, Isaac, and Jacob
Is the same God that takes care of us
Through all our pain, sick days and strife
He continues to give us a decent life
Although there are things I cannot see
I have confidence in His word and still believe
His Son and Spirit are also alive
They give us comfort
to help us survive
I'm grateful for the change
He has made in me
He deserves all of our love,
praise, honor, and glory

Galations 3:9
So then they that be of faith
are blessed with faithful Abraham.

Jesus Cares

John 8:12
Then spake Jesus again unto them, saying, "I am the light of the
world: he that followeth me shall not walk in darkness,
but shall have the light of life"

Thank You Lord for loving me
For giving Your life that I might be free
For giving me a chance to save my soul
Through the Father's words one can be whole
Thank You for living a life that's true
Sharing and caring that we might follow You
Showing the way to eternal life
Teaching one how to overcome strife
Lord thank You for forgiving my sins
Thank You for staying with me till this life ends
And after this life I know You will be
The one that keeps me through eternity

Joy Over Sorrow

John 14:16
And I will pray the Father,
and he shall give you another comforter
that he may abide with you forever.

God gives us blessings every day
We should enjoy them before they are taken away
Enjoy your family and circle of friends
Good times and accept things when life's road bends
We never can know what lies ahead
But our faith can stay strong
because of what we've read
Jesus our Savior lived His life
Solving problems and teaching what's right
We need to believe and learn to obey
Trusting God and knowing His Son is the way
To a brighter future filled with peace and love
In our heavenly home prepared up above
And when God says it's time to come home
Remember those who are left are never alone

Job 1:21b
The Lord gave, and the Lord hath taketh away;
blessed be the name of the Lord.

Keeping The Faith

James 4:10
Humble yourselves in the sight of the Lord,
and he shall lift you up.

There are blessings all around us
floating in the air
And one with your name on it
for Jesus put it there
When you're a child of God
the highest of all Kings
His only Son can help you
with stress and everything
With all of life's problems
when you don't know what to do
Until things get better Jesus will comfort you
God's word can have a soothing effect
that relax yet stimulates
They open up your mind and heart
and give you a way to escape
So take the hand of Jesus and hold it very tight
Keep praying that your faith stays strong
morning noon and night
When Satan comes to tempt you
don't let him turn you around
Say these words LEAVE ME ALONE
because I'm Heaven Bound

James 4:7
Submit yourselves therefore to God;
resist the devil and he will flee from you.

Lasting Friendship

Colossians 3:17
And whatsoever ye do in word or deed,
do all in the name of the Lord Jesus,
giving thanks to God and the Father by him.

It's not how long you've known them
It's not how often you see them
It's only important to know they are there
By the way they act you know they care
A smile or a hug goes a long long way
Sometimes we need them to make our day
So treat your friends with kindness and love
Through the Holy Spirit sent from above
And keep God's word within your heart
So no one can tear your friendship apart

Learning To Live

Matthew 6:33
But seek ye first the kingdom of God, and His
righteousness: and all things shall be added unto you.

A greater appreciation of life to share
I've learned there's always someone who cares
He never sleeps whether night or day
He gave us guidelines to show the way
His word is truth His way is fair
He gives us love teaches us to care

While on this earth with temptations and trials
It gets rough sometimes yet I'm able to smile
It's because of our Savior Gods only Son
He has shown us how the victory is won
To walk in the light and do what is right
Is not so hard to do
The way to a good life is in God's Word
I found it and so can you

Legacy of Love

1 John 4:7
Beloved, let us love one another; for love is of God;
And everyone that loveth is born of God, and knoweth God.

We stand on many shoulders
of people down the line
They passed on the word of God
who is loving and kind
We are told of the generations
that helped make our way
And taught us how to appreciate
our good and even bad days
They made life easier for us to bear
There were many dark days they had to share
But thanks be to God
who brought them through
So they could make life
better for me and you
Now let us stand together
with love and pride
And pray for God's Spirit to stay by our side
Be sure to thank Jesus for shedding His blood
Follow His footsteps and show others love

1 John 4:11
Beloved if God so loved us, we ought also to love one another.

Living Through Christ

Joshua 24:15a
And if it seem evil unto you to serve the Lord,
choose ye this day whom ye will serve.

I hope from my life someone will say
I was able to help show them the way
To the joy and peace that I have found
In God's holy word and from searching around
Following Jesus God's only son
Is the way this Christian race is won

I hope my life will be an arrow
To point to the road that's straight and narrow
To receive the gift of salvation there
That was set aside because God truly cares
I pray that God will work through me
So others will live eternally
And if through me that work does show
I know I'll be able to enter Heaven's door

Look For Tomorrow

Psalms 9:10
And they that know thy name will put thy trust in thee
For thou Lord, has not forsaken them that seek thee.

I believe in my heart God knows what's best
And we have to try to withstand the test
We don't have to face them all alone
Through the life of Christ
we've already been shown
He gives joy when you're sad
His peace can make you glad
And in time your wounds will heal
Pray for strength to endure
for I'm very sure
The word of God is real

Philippians 4:7
And the peace of God, which passeth all understanding,
shall keep your hearts and minds through Christ Jesus.

Mending Our Ways

Matthew 7:1
Judge not, that ye be not judged.

My name is not Paula Perfect
I know I'm not always right
But I try to do the best I can
for I'm always in God's sight
God says we should love one another
be kind and say what's true
Judging is His territory
it's not for us to do
So lend a helping hand
to one who needs it most
And give God all the credit
for it's not for us to boast

My Best Choice

Joshua 24:15a
And if it seem evil unto you to serve the Lord,
choose ye this day whom ye will serve.

There are choices to be made in this earthly life
I'm glad I was led to the right table
I've learned about real love and sacrifice
And that Jesus God's Son is able
He's able to sit by His Father's side
Able to plead our case
For He experienced heartache and pain
Things in this life we must face
Through trial and error we learn each day
How our lives can be stable
I pray like me you make the right choice
And accept God's word from His table
And as you grow older when life seem to change
Sometimes it may take awhile
Be grateful and praise the Father and Son
And thank Him for being His child

Joshua 24:15 b
But as for me and my house, we will serve the Lord.

Our True And Living God

Ephesians 4:6
One God and Father of all,
who is above all, and through all,
and in you all.

Our God is known as the great I Am
He gave us a gift of His perfect Lamb
The Lamb is Jesus our Savior from sin
God's only Son and our best friend
He tells us to pray to our Father above
For He gives grace mercy and genuine love
God is the one that forgives our wrong ways
He gave us a guide to brighten our days
Even through heartache sickness and pain
His written word assures us we have much to gain
A place in His Kingdom with His Son by His side
And His Holy Spirit our Comforter and Guide

Revelation 22:14
Blessed are they that do his commandments,
that they may have the right to the tree of life,
and may enter in through the gates into the city.

Our BFF From God
(Best Friend Forever)

Psalms 116:12
What shall I render unto the Lord for all his benefits toward me?

God gave us our Best Friend Forever
His name is Jesus Christ
He knows about our burdens
For he shared them throughout His life
He took our sins upon Himself a way to set us free
He left a testimony to help us with our needs
There are many things we go through
While we're here upon this earth
But nothing like His mother had after giving birth
He lived His life to teach us
things that we should do
I always look unto the hills
for the joy that carries me through
And since this is a brand new day
with new blessings from above
I'm grateful that we have this Friend
That gives us peace and love

Our Christmas Gift From God

Psalm105:1
O give thanks unto the Lord; call upon his name:
make known his deeds among the people.

God gave us a special Christmas gift
His name is Jesus Christ
He was born to save us from our sins
And a chance to have new life
We still celebrate His birthday
After more than two thousand years
And thank Him for sharing His Spirit
Who always will be near
It's time to praise and worship Him
And let others feel His love
We should always be grateful to our God
Who still reigns from Heaven above

Paying Rent With Good Deeds

John 13:35
By this shall all men know that ye are my disciples,
if ye have love one to another.

We are all tenants on this earth
living from day to day
And before it's time for us to move
We should try to improve our ways
As we look forward to the new earth
Jesus' gift of salvation a brand new birth
We should keep Gods word close in our heart
It's the strength we need so we won't depart
None of us are greater
than our Sisters or Brothers
So let us join hands and love one another
Our God sits high He sees all that we do
His Son is coming back for us
because His word is true
And we will answer for all we did wrong
And hope God will say with Him we belong

Prayer Is The Key

Ecclesiastes 3:17
I said in mine heart, God shall judge the righteous and the wicked:
for there is a time for every purpose and for every work.

Hatred is like an all-consuming fire
Makes you say and do all kinds of things
But remember to pray to our almighty God
and see how much peace He can bring
He can put your enemies on their knees
He can toss them to and fro
He can make them regret whatever was done
no matter where they go
But for your life He can take your strife
and make you smile again
He can comfort your heart
that's been torn apart
For all battles He can win
So keep your trust and faith in God
in all the things you do
For He always extends
His love, grace, and mercy
He's the one that will see you through

Psalms 138:7
Though I walk in the midst of trouble, thou wilt revive me:
thou shalt stretch forth thy hand against the wrath of my enemies,
and thy right hand shall save me.

Preparing Our Hearts And Minds

2 Corinthians 5:1
For we know that if our earthly house of this tabernacle were dissolved,
we have a building of God, an house not made with hands,
eternal in the heavens.

Be ye ever so grateful,
there's no place like home
A home God prepared
for His children alone
A place full of love
where there's no need for tears
A place where there will be
no heartaches or fears
Jesus our savior knows the way
His Spirit guides us every day
If we keep our minds on heavenly things
Our Souls will rejoice
our hearts will sing
So keep the faith and one day we'll be
In that home with all things
God wants us to see

Searching For Peace

Ecclesiastes 12:10
The preacher sought to find out acceptable words:
and that which was written was upright,
even words of truth.

While you're traveling
on your yellow brick road
To find the King of Kings
You must always read the word of God
And try to understand what it means
If you have a Pastor
to help guide your way
He can open your eyes
and brighten your days
There will always be blocks
and cracks in the road
Just remember God's words
can lighten your load
So when troubles arise
and jump in your face
Quote scripture from the Bible
and continue your race
You will not only find the King of Kings
But all the joy that He can bring

Seeing God With The Eyes Of The Heart

Job 42:5
I have heard of thee by the hearing of the ear;
but now mine eye seeth thee.

Because I believe in what I've read and heard
Hearing the scriptures and reading Your word
My life has new meaning because Jesus was here
To show all the people He truly cares
God allowed Him to die on the cross just for us
To show in our lifetime the one we could trust
He then took Him home to live by His side
And inspired His Disciples to write us a guide
We will always need Jesus from day to day
For we never know what may come our way
So thank you for giving us so much love
And the undeserved blessings you send from above
The eyes of my heart can see what you do
And know that Your words are honest and true
And if we live right, we have nothing to fear
For one day we'll be where there's no more tears

Revelation7:17
For the Lamb which is in the midst of the throne
shall feed them, and shall lead them unto living
fountains of water; and God shall wipe away
all tears from their eyes.

Sharing God's Light

Matthew 5:16
Let your light so shine before men,
that they may see your good works,
and glorify your Father which is in heaven.

I may not be perfect in man's eyesight
But God still sees me as His child
His patience and love paid off in my life
Even though it took quite a while
One thing that's important in our new lives
Should be how we treat one another
Remembering to live the best we can
Showing God's love to our Sisters and Brothers

The Father, Son and Holy Spirit,
Three who work as one
And we that read the written word
Should make sure their work is done
There's no guarantee we will always succeed
To help other people believe
But we must do our best to past life's test
Giving to those we know are in need

Stop, Look, And Listen

Ephesians 4:32
And be ye kind one to another, tenderhearted, forgiving one another,
even as God for Christ sake hath forgiven you.

We don't always remember
the things we've said or done
But each new day we're here on earth
our future has begun
What Jesus did on Calvary
is sad but yet it's true
How He gave His life to save
all sinners like me and you
But God said wait it's not the end
We still have work to do
So all the people that hear our words
will know that they are true
We will send Preachers to teach
and show my people the way
To let them know there is a price
for what they do and say
Now we as Christian people
should treat our neighbors right
And know whatever path we choose
we're always in God's sight
There may be times we go astray
and slip off the right path
That's why we have God's armor
to help complete our task
Praise God and give Him glory
for all the things He's done
Thank Him for His Holy Spirit
and His Wonderful Matchless Son

73

Strength To Endure

Philippians 4:13
I can do all things
through Christ which strengtheneth me.

Through trials and tribulations
The questions always asked
Why me Lord, why me?
But trials make you stronger
if you learn how to trust
In God whom you cannot see
Though your head may hang low
life seems at an end
Look to Jesus where life truly begins
It's when faith takes hold
God makes you content
With a peace and joy
that can only be sent
So when trouble arise
you need strength to bear
Remember Jesus Christ
is the one who truly cares

Philippians 4:11
For I have learned in whatsoever state I am,
therewith to be content.

Striving For Perfection

Colossians 3:17
And whatsoever ye do in word or deed,
do all in the name of the Lord Jesus,
giving thanks to God and the Father by him.

God put His love within us
To show He truly cares
Jesus lived His life to show us
How to treat each other fair
The Holy Spirit reminds us
Of all that we should do
To share and show our lives have changed
And we have become brand new
Although we're not perfected
God's work is not yet done
But keep the faith and always remember
The sacrifice of His Son

Philippians 2:5
Let this mind be in you.
which was also in Christ Jesus.

Take A Look

Psalms145:9
The Lord is good to all; and his
tender mercies are over all his works.

Look in the mirror what do you see
Look in the mirror who do you see
When I look at the what, I see me
When I look at the who
I see a child of the King
And then I know I have everything
Things like love, and forgiveness of sin
Grace and mercy, peace within
Joy, when things are not going right
I can keep moving forward morning and night
I'm glad I can look past just seeing me
And look to the hills to the one I believe
God our Father and Jesus His Son
Taught us how this worldly race is won
His Holy Spirit, our comforter and guide
Continues to lead us and stay by our side
So as you look in the mirror
Go past what you see
And thank God for His grace
And undeserved mercy

Take Hold

1 Corinthians 15:22
For as in Adam all die,
even so in Christ shall all be made alive

There's a lifeline connected to Christ
He is the way to salvation
The only true friend
in time of need
The one that brings resurrection
He holds the key that unlocks the door
To the path that leads to the streets of gold
He's the tie that binds
He's the peace within
He's the one that loves
He forgives our sins
And when your time on earth is through
He has new life waiting for you

Take Some Time Out

Psalms 34:8
O taste and see that the Lord is good;
blessed is the man that trusted in Him.

There's so much beauty in the world
If you look beyond the evil to see it
There's so much joy and love in the world
If you know the source that supplies it
There is a rainbow after the rain
Real joy and peace comes after your pain
There's no true love without Christ in your life
Just try Him and see what I mean
He can lift you up if you open your mind
He can give you strength through trying times
It's not much effort just learn His words
Through all life's confusion
His voice can be heard
So take a minute, stop and relax
Find out what's important to you
And be sure to put Jesus God's only Son
In the center of all you do

The Best Place To Be

Psalm 16:11
Thou will show me the path of life;
in thy presence is fullness and joy ;
At thy right hand there are pleasures forevermore .

In the presence of the Lord
is the best place to be
I'm glad He's available at all times
He makes your days and nights complete
He gives you peace of mind
He lifts your spirit when you're feeling down
For He knows when things go wrong
He lets you feel Him by your side
When everyone else is gone
I thank God for His kindness and love
For taking an interest in me
I thank Him for being who He is
And allowing my eyes to see
What my heart tells me has always been true
That the life God gives
is exciting and new

The Lasting Love Of God

Psalms 18:1
I will love thee, O Lord, my strength.

Through all the ups and downs in life
The love of God still stands
His love takes you through trying times
While His Spirit holds your hand
God always tells us how we should act
In His written word He left for us
It tells how to build and have faith in Him
For He's the one to trust
His kind of love can give you strength
When people let you down
And the comforter that Jesus left is always around
I know you never see Him
but he's present anyway
And when you ask for help you'll see
He will brighten up your day
So if you get sad or lonely
remember you're always loved
By our Father and His Son Jesus
who sends it from above

Psalms 16:11
Thou wilt shew me the path of life;
in thy presence is fullness of joy;
at thy right hand there are pleasures forevermore.

The Lord Will Provide

Psalm 38 :21
Forsake me not, O Lord;
O my God, be not far from me.

God humbles us in so many ways
He works through people to brighten our days
He's always there to hear our cry
He'll even answer when we ask why
Why in my life is there so much rain
Why do I have to have this pain
In time He will let the clouds pass by
And through His word He will answer our why's
And when He comes to take us home
Our Shepherd says we are not alone
Praise God stay close to Him through prayer
And let others know He truly cares
Remember He's always by our side
And He's willing and able to provide

Psalm 34 :1
I will bless the Lord at all times;
His praise shall continually be in my mouth

The Love Of The Trinity

1 Corinthians 2:12
Now we have received not the Spirit of the world;
but the Spirit which is of God; that we might know
the things that are freely given to us of God;

The Cross of Jesus is in my heart
The Cross is in my mind
I know I'll never stray because
I know He's one of a kind
No one is as humble
No one is as true
No one can give us new life
that's honest and new
And when life seems empty
and no one can be found
I keep my head toward the sky
instead of looking down
Thank You, Lord for all the things
You have done in the past
You hung on the cross for sinners
until You completed Your task
All praise, glory, and honor
to the Father and Son
Your Holy Spirit shows us
we're blessed by three in one

The Narrow Road

James2:8
If ye fulfill the royal law according to the scripture,
Thou shalt love thy neighbor as thyself
ye do well.

Jesus keep me near the cross
I need to stay close so I won't get lost
It's easy today to step out of line
The Bible forewarned us
about living in these times
All kinds of temptation we see everyday
So we must follow Jesus
for He's the only way
A way to our Father who sits high above
In spite of our sins
He still offers love
But it won't last forever
His mercy and grace
So let's share His love with others
while we're running this race

James 5:8
Be ye also patient; establish your hearts:
for the coming of the Lord draweth nigh.

The Sacrificed Lamb Of God

Revelation 3:21
To him that overcometh will I grant to sit with me
in my throne, even as I also overcame,
and am set down with my Father in his throne

On Good Friday we remember
what Jesus did for us
He gave His life to show all people
In God we need to trust
But early Sunday morning
God said get up my Son
It's time you come back home with Me
Your race you truly won
You had your share of sorrow
Sometime you even cried
Now come and take your rightful place
Here by My right side
If we follow in His footsteps
Jesus said He'll lead the way
Where we can be around God's throne
For by grace our souls have been saved

John 10:11
I am the good shepherd; the good shepherd
giveth his life for the sheep.

The Words Of My Mouth

Psalms 119:169
Let my cry come near before thee, O Lord;
give me understanding according to thy word.

I pray to the Lord to answer the prayers
that are on my mind and heart
I know in order to get results
I have to do my part
My part is to treat all people right
regardless of their race, weight or height
And even if we disagree
God's word is the answer if you believe
We have the right to choose our path
for God gave us all free will
And His Holy Spirit will guide us
when we listen and be still
The main thing that we see these days
is confusion all around us
But Jesus said these times would come
just keep your faith and trust
So I will continue to pray
for you and others everywhere
And try to follow God's Holy Spirit
because I truly care

Psalms 90:12
Teach us to number our days,
that we may apply our hearts unto wisdom.

The World Is Also God's House

Proverbs 25:28
He that hath no rule over his own spirit
is like a city that is broken down
and without walls.

When we live in God's house He can live inside of us
We should play by his rules for He's the one to trust
When we think we know it all and go on our own
We lose His protection He leaves us alone
But that doesn't mean He turns His back on you
It's only to show you will miss what He can do
There are lessons to be learned each and every day
We follow Jesus' teaching for He is the way
The way to handle stress, heartache, and pain
Through all life's issues never forget His name
He sacrificed His life for us and hung on the cross
For hours He suffered so we would not be lost
He opened the door to His Father's house
Invited all to come in
He gave us the key His written word
To show us where to begin
We have His rules to follow
His Spirit to keep us strong
And it's up to us to choose our path
One's right, the other wrong
So keep your mind on Jesus
And all that He has done
Tell others about the Father's house
And the joy you have won

The World Today

Hebrews 8:12
For I will be merciful to their unrighteousness,
and their sins and their iniquities
will I remember no more.

We never completely understand
some things we must go through
But when you look at the world today
you know God's word is true
Things are so much different
than what they were before
So if you need to change your ways
Jesus still stands at the door
He waits for you to invite Him in
to help you change your ways
Along with His Holy Spirit
they will brighten up your days
You then can hold up God's banner
and do the best you can
Trusting and believing one day
You will live in God's promised new land

Think Before You Speak

James 3:18
And the fruit of righteousness
is sown in peace and them that make peace.

Sometimes things are said
through anger or stress
But if we hold our tongues
we can pass a test
God rewards those
who try to keep peace
So watch your tongue
until anger cease
We say we don't mean
whatever comes out
But others that hear us
have their doubts
So let God's Spirit
control the things you say
For you never know who's
in need of a brighter better day

Through Pain And Sorrow

Psalms 120:1
In my distress I cried unto the Lord,
and he heard me.

My pain is almost too much to bear
Lord I know You're around and I know You care
There are things in life we must go through
You say hold on I'll strengthen you
It seems the pain will never go away
But when I look to the hills
I can see better days
Your comforting Spirit helps me believe
Then I'm able to sleep and get some relief
Dear God I give You all the glory
Thank Your Son and Spirit too
If I did not have You in my life
I don't know what I would do
I hope I can encourage
Someone else who has pain
That God will send His sunshine
And remove the clouds and rain

Psalms 121:1
I will lift up mine eyes unto the hills,
from whence cometh my help.

Through The Years

Psalm 139:1
O Lord thou hast searched me,
and known me.

I will bless the Lord
With my heart and soul
He has kept me all these years
He blessed me when I didn't know Him
When I was full of doubt and fears
But since He came into my life
I am able to handle
Disappointment and strife
I know what it means to love and be loved
I've learned all good things
Come from above
I thank my God with all that's in me
For He made me the woman
He knew I could be

Psalm 139:14
I will praise thee; for I am fearfully and
wonderfully made: Marvelous are thy works;
and that my soul knoweth right well.

Today Is Important

Matthew 6:34
Take therefore no thought for the morrow.
For the morrow shall take thought
for the things of itself.
Sufficient unto the day is the evil thereof.

Tomorrow is not promised to us
For it's always a day away
So since we live a day at a time
We should watch what we do and say
God gives a list to show us,
The things that's right and wrong
And through His grace and mercy
We should know where we belong
Today we need to praise His name
For tomorrow may never come
But we have a Savior named Jesus
God's precious number one Son
Let's not forget His Holy Spirit
Who is here to comfort us
So today we still have a chance to say
In God we put our trust

Together In Christ

Philippians 1:27
Only let your conversation be as it becometh
the gospel of Christ; that ye stand fast
in one spirit, with one mind,
striving together for the faith of the gospel

All for one, and one for all
Should always be our theme
Like the Father, Son, and Holy Spirit
We should be a special team
Working together hand in hand
Our goals should be the same
Always praying for one another
In love, and in Jesus name
When we lift our voice to praise our God
Our praise should be from our hearts
But how can we praise Him together
When we're standing so far apart
The kindness God has shown us
We're supposed to pass it on
And except His gift of eternal life
That was purchased by His Son

Treating Others With Godly Ways

Psalms 117:1
O praise the Lord, all ye nations;
praise him all ye people.

My praise to God is how I live,
and treat you everyday
My love for Christ is how I try
to help show you the way
The way that leads to a better life
filled with joy and love
The peace of mind that only comes
from our God who lives above
Our hectic life on earth each day
can tear us all apart
It's why we need the love of God
stored within our hearts
And then we will remember how
to treat each other right
And keep in mind whatever we do
we're always in God's sight

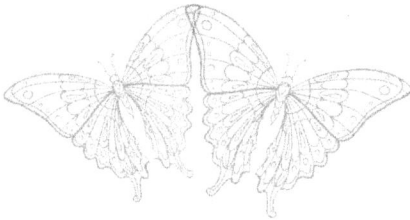

Walking In Truth

1 Samuel 12:24
Only fear the Lord, and serve him in truth
with all your heart: for consider how
great things he has done for you.

The only way to please our God
Is in spirit and in truth
Hide His word within your heart
So it can grow and take root
Our lives won't be perfect
For our human side will show
But we won't stray too far off the path
For God's Spirit won't let us go
Hold on to the word of truth
And let it guide your way
Be kind to one another
As you live from day to day

T - The beginning of trust
R - We read God's Word
U- Applies to all of us
T - For teaching others
H -For heaven where we will all meet again

Wealth That Gives Peace

Matthew 11:28
Come unto me, all ye that labour and are
heavy laden. and I will give you rest.

In your older years when it seems no one cares
Jesus is there for our burdens to bear
When your life seems heavy
Due to failing health
Our Father in Heaven has all the wealth
Wealth that can cure or ease your pain
Wealth that insures you have something to gain
A place in God's Kingdom prepared for us
Through Jesus Christ whom we always can trust
Wealth that's beyond the years you have lived
The power of love is God's gift to give
Wealth is not always money you see
It can touch your heart if you only believe
So when sadness seems to cloud your mind
Reach out for Jesus He's one of a kind

When You Feel Alone

Psalm 25:17
The troubles of my heart are enlarged;
O bring thou me out of my distresses.

When you're all alone and not feeling right
Think of Jesus and His great sacrifice
Who are we and what do we give
We can only show love
Through the life that we live
No need for self-pity, feeling down and out
For God's grace alone is a reason to shout
The love that was shown on Calvary
The blood that was shed for you and me
It's a gift of life for us to share
And to know there's always
Someone who cares
So keep in mind remember you are not alone
God's Holy Spirit gives you comfort
Until Jesus takes you home

Psalm 121:1
I will lift up mine eyes unto the hills,
from whence cometh my help.

Where Is Your Focus?

Psalms 118:8
It is better to trust in the Lord
than to put confidence in man.

Your focus should always be on Christ
not on your sisters and brothers
For He's the one that will lead you right
He's stronger and better than others
He has the power to forgive our sins
and help us along our way
You don't have to guess how you should act
or what you should do or say
God's Holy Spirit will guide you
through life's ifs, whens, and whys
So keep your mind on the life of Christ
and your eyes up to the sky
Our sky should be the bible
inspired by Gods own words
And we should take some time to read
what we have already heard

Psalms 119:105
Thy word is a lamp unto my feet,
and a light unto my path.

Where Joy Is Found

Psalm 19:8
The statutes of the Lord are right,
The commandments of the Lord are pure,
enlightening the eyes.

If you reach out and let Jesus make your way
You'll enjoy your life from day to day
If you reach for the sky
You'll be surprised to find
A loving spirit that's warm gentle and kind
It's the Spirit of God and His loving Son
The Spirit that joins us together as one
One family united is what we should be
It's what God our creator wants to see
So reach for the sky where blessings flow
Where prayers are answered
And you're promised much more

Wisdom And Understanding

Proverbs 4:11
I have taught thee in the way of wisdom;
I have led thee in right paths.

Common Sense has a name, his name is Holy Spirit
He guides us to God's written word
and all the love that's in it
It tells how we were born in sin
but God gave us an out
He sacrificed His only son
whom we should praise and not doubt
Eternal freedom is what He gives
a chance to live beyond our years
A place where we will shed no tears
Free from pain away from our fears
Listen to the good voice in your heart and head
Remember Jesus hung on the cross for us and bled
He now reigns by His Father's side
and Common Sense is still our guide

Proverbs 4:7
Wisdom is the principle thing; therefore get wisdom:
and with all thy getting get understanding.

A Letter to God
You Were Always There

Psalm 24:1
The earth is the Lords, and the fullness thereof;
The world and they that dwell therein

Father, You have always been in my life
I just didn't know you were there
But looking back I know I've been blessed
Someone stronger than family cared
I know who has been my helping hand
Since my family left me behind
They knew I would have the best of care
From the one who is loving and kind
Whenever I cry You wipe my tears
And bring me out of whatever I fear
For our time on earth is not always the best
But you give us hope in time of stress
So thank You for being the one we can trust
For Your comforting Spirit, who stays close to us
For Your only Son who died on the cross
To open our eyes so we won't be lost

Psalm 27:1
The Lord is my light and my salvation;
whom shall I fear?
The Lord is the strength of my life;
of whom shall I be afraid?

Thoughts from the author...
Carmen L. Howard

SHARED THOUGHTS AND FEELINGS

THOUGHTS FROM THE AUTHOR

Looking within my life, I was 15 years old when my mother passed away. My grandmother, who we lovingly called Grams, tried to give the best spiritual guidance she had, but her words never seemed to soak in until the merry-go-round I put myself on kept spinning round and round. Finally I said "I need a change, GOD HELP ME!" Only then did I really try to learn who God is, and why he allowed his only Son to die for us sinners. I learned why Jesus was willing to give His life for us. I learned what true love is all about. All the things I looked for in people, I was able to find in the word of God.

My peace, my joy, my thoughts and feelings are in the pages I shared with you.

To my children, as Peter said in Acts 3:6, "Silver and gold have I none but such as I have give I thee."(KJV)

A proper ending for my book is like the humble beginning. Giving all praises to the Father- God, the Son- Jesus, and His Holy Spirit. Thank you for lifting me up and giving me the desire and a chance to share your love.

Carmen Howard and The Holy Spirit in Me!